Learning Yo
Hanja: Beginner's Guide to
Reading and Writing
Korean Chinese Characters

By Jieun Yoo

Table of Contents

Preface

Introduction to Hanja

Your First 20 Hanja

Additional Notes on Characters

Exercises

Answer Key

Preface

If you started studying Korean, you probably have encountered hanja in some form. To deeply appreciate the nuances of the language, learning hanja is crucial. Further, Hanja themselves are still used in newspapers, advertisements, restaurant menus, and on storefront billboards, so you will need to master them if you want to be fully literate in Korean.

Many Korean language books do not teach hanja until after you are at an advanced level, or only teach it as an elective. But, learning hanja is not difficult at all. Once you learn the basics, you will be able to extend your knowledge through self-study. This book starts you out with your first twenty hanja, which are some of the simplest hanja used.

You will learn how to write and pronounce the hanja as well as their English and Korean meanings. In particular, the stroke order for writing each character is clearly indicated. After reading this book, you will be well on your way to recognizing and using these hanja in your daily life in Korea!

Introduction to Hanja

The Korean alphabet is called Hangul. It was created a long time ago during the Joseon dynasty. All words can be expressed using the Hangul alphabet, so hanja is not technically needed in writing.

Hanja are Chinese characters that are used in a Korean way. Even though the Korean alphabet can phonetically express all sounds, some Korean words have Chinese roots and can be expressed using Chinese characters. For these words, there is a separate and distinct Korean meaning and pronunciation for the Chinese characters used. In other words, even if the character used in Korea is also used in China, there is a unique Korean pronunciation of the character.

As mentioned, pure Hangul can always be used. However, it is still useful to know the roots behind some Korean words that are based on Chinese characters. Understanding Hanja will help one become more literate in Korean.

Further, some books, advertisements, newspapers, restaurant menus, storefront billboards, etc. still use hanja, so it's helpful to know the basic characters in your daily life.

In this book, you will learn the following hanja:

一 二 三 四 五

六 七 八 九 十

小 中 大 月 日

山 木 人 火 水

They will probably look foreign to you if you have never studied hanja. However, if you have lived in Korea or studied Korean, you may have seen some of these characters and wondered about their meanings and how to write them.

These hanja are beginning level hanja, which are "Level 8" hanja. There are 9 levels of hanja - from Level 0 through Level 8 (Levels 0, 1, 2, 3, 4, 5, 6, 7, 8).

Level 8 hanja are composed of fifty basic hanja, which are learned in elementary school. These are the basic hanja that you need to get started in your studies. This book introduces you to 20 of the most basic hanja; future volumes in this series will introduce you to more of the characters. As you progress in the series, you will be able to go from recognizing simple hanja to being able to put them together in words.

Each hanja is itself composed of a number of smaller elments called radicals. These are the parts that make up the character. When writing hanja, you should follow some basic rules. You should start at the top of the character and work your way down in writing the stroke. Also, your writing strokes should go from left to right.

The sample hanja in this book show you the stroke order needed. For example, each radical is written with one stroke, and they should be written in order, for example, follow the sequence indicated by the arrows 1, 2, 3, etc. Further, each individually numbered stroke as shown in the ensuing pages should be written without lifting up your pen, as some radicals are not just simple lines.

For each hanja, the English meaning is given. Then, the Korean pronunciation of the character as well as the native word for the character is given. The first hanja that you will learn is the character 一 . This is the character that means "one". The Korean pronunciation for this character is "il" (일) and the native Korean word for "one" here is "han" (한).

Koreans themselves learn the meanings and pronunciations of Chinese characters in that way, for example, they would learn that the hanja which is symbolized by 一 is pronounced il and means the native Korean word han, which means one.

Note for more advanced learners

If you are a more advanced learner, you should memorize the hanja thus as "Han, il (한 일)" as they are memorized in Korean as such. There are different words that symbolize the meaning "one." In the case of learning hanja here, "han" is the typical memorized word. In speaking Korean, you may use other words depending on the context.

Your First 20 Hanja

Writing Tips

Writing Tip!
Start from the left
and draw the stroke
from left to right

1

English Meaning: One

Korean Sound: 일 (il)

Korean Meaning: 한 (1)

Hangul for the
Korean Sound

Pronounced
in English as
"il"

English Meaning: One
Korean Sound: 일 (il)
Korean Meaning: 한 (1)

English Meaning: Two
Korean Sound: 이 **(e)**
Korean Meaning: 두 **(2)**

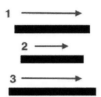

English Meaning: Three
Korean Sound: 삼 (sam)
Korean Meaning: 석(3)

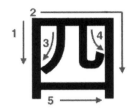

English Meaning: Four
Korean Sound: 사 (sa)
Korean Meaning: 넉 (4)

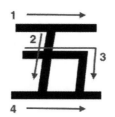

English Meaning: Five
Korean Sound: 오 (o)
Korean Meaning: 다섯(5)

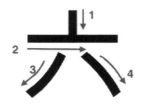

English Meaning: Six
Korean Sound: 육 (yuk)
Korean Meaning: 여섯 (6)

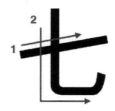

English Meaning: Seven
Korean Sound: 칠 (chil)
Korean Meaning: 일곱 (7)

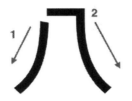

English Meaning: Eight
Korean Sound: 팔 (pal)
Korean Meaning: 여덟 (8)

English Meaning: Nine
Korean Sound: 구 (ku)
Korean Meaning: 아홉 (9)

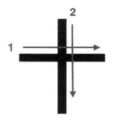

English Meaning: Ten
Korean Sound: 십 (ship)
Korean Meaning: 열 (10)

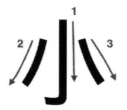

English Meaning: Small
Korean Sound: 소 (so)
Korean Meaning: 작을

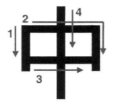

English Meaning: Middle
Korean Sound: 중(joong)
Korean Meaning: 가운데

English Meaning: Large
Korean Sound: 대 (dae)
Korean Meaning: 큰

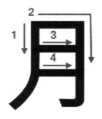

English Meaning: Moon, Month
Korean Sound: 월 (wol)
Korean Meaning: 달

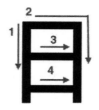

English Meaning: Day
Korean Sound: 일 (il)
Korean Meaning: 날 (nal)

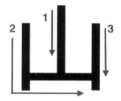

English Meaning: Mountain
Korean Sound: 산(san)
Korean Meaning: 메

English Meaning: Tree
Korean Sound: 목 (mok)
Korean Meaning: 나무

English Meaning: Person
Korean Sound: 인 (in)
Korean Meaning: 사람

English Meaning: Fire
Korean Sound: 화(hwa)
Korean Meaning: 불

English Meaning: Water
Korean Sound: 수 (su)
Korean Meaning: 물

Additional Notes on Characters

The first ten characters you learned, 一 二 三 四 五 六 七 八 九 十 represent the numbers 1 through 10.

The next three characters, 小 中 大 mean small, medium, and large, respectively. The character 中 can also mean middle. 中 is the character used in the word "middle school." 大 is the character used for the word university.

The next two characters you learned were 月 and 日. 月 literally means "moon" and it can also mean "month" as well. 日 means day. You can write days of the year as 1 月 2 日, which would mean January 2nd. Literally, it translates as the first month of the year and the 2nd day of that month.

You will notice that the character for the number one, 一 has the same sound as the character for the word day, 日. Both of them are pronounced 일 ("il"). Usually, Koreans can tell which word the sound indicates from the context of the word. Once in awhile, particularly in cases of technical writing, there might be some ambiguity – this is why it pays to know the Chinese characters behind the pronunciations. Some more academic books will write the Korean word in Hangul, and then the Chinese characters for the word in parentheses.

山 if you recall means "mountain" and 木 means "tree."

人 is the character for "person" and can also mean in general "human being."

火 is the character for "fire" and 水 is the character for "water."

Finally, please note that the above characters are the usual, print versions of the characters. Individuals have their own writing styles, so you may see very slight variations in calligraphic writing styles when you see these characters outside of printed text.

Exercises

The answers to these exercises are at the end of the book.

Write the number each character represents.

1) 一

2) 二

3) 三

4) 四

5) 五

6) 六

7) 七

8) 八

9) 九

10) 十

11) 七

12) 一

13) 二

14) 四

15) 五

16) 八

17) 九

18) 十

19) 六

20) 三

21) Which one is in order: Small, Medium, Large?
A) 小 大 中
B) 小 中 大
C) 大 中 小

22) Choose the character that represents the number 6.
A) 大
B) 人
C) 六
D) 水

23) Choose the number that is largest.
A) 七
B) 三
C) 四
D) 五

24) Choose the smallest number.
A) 八
B) 九
C) 十
D) 四

25) Which character would you use to put out a fire?
A) 火
B) 水
C) 山
D) 四

26) If you had to buy a "medium-sized" shirt, and signs were written in hanja, which character would get you the right size?
A) 小
B) 中
C) 大

27) Three plus one = ?
A) 二
B) 六
C) 十
D) 四

28) 九 minus 一 equals?
A) 四
B) 八
C) 五
D) 六

29) There are many _____ at a _____.
A) 山,木
B) 木, 山
C) 月, 火
D) 大, 山

30) The character used for month is ?
A) 小
B) 中
C) 日
D) 月

31) The character used for day is ?
A) 日
B) 小
C) 七
D) 月

32) This character is used in the Korean word for Middle School.
A) 三
B) 中
C) 日
D) 人

33) Which character is not a number?
A) 六
B) 大
C) 五
D) 十

34) 二 times 四 equals ?
A) 五
B) 十
C) 三
D) 八

35) Which character represents the number of main directions on a compass?
A) 二
B) 四
C) 六
D) 九

36) Which character represents person?
A) 大
B) 八
C) 人
D) 水

37) 七 plus 一 plus 一 plus 一 equals ?
A) 八
B) 七
C) 十
D) 六

38) Which character means "large"?
A) 四
B) 大
C) 月
D) 九

39) The oceans are made of this character.
A) 火
B) 水
C) 小
D) 日

40) There are 12 _____ in a year.

A) 月

B) 中

C) 四

D) 日

41) Match the Chinese character with its Korean pronunciation: 大

A) 일

B) 중

C) 산

D) 대

42) Match the Chinese character with its Korean pronunciation: 六

A) 소

B) 십

C) 육

D) 화

43) Match the Chinese character with its Korean pronunciation: 四

A) 사

B) 오

C) 육

D) 수

44) Match the Chinese character with its Korean pronunciation: 十
  A) 십
  B) 수
  C) 오
  D) 대

45) Match the Chinese character with its Korean pronunciation: 木
  A) 인
  B) 화
  C) 목
  D) 구

46) Match the Chinese character with its Korean pronunciation: 人
  A) 인
  B) 삼
  C) 사
  D) 중

47) Match the Chinese character with its Korean pronunciation: 水
  A) 월
  B) 이
  C) 수
  D) 소

48) Match the Chinese character with its Korean pronunciation: 九
    A) 칠
    B) 구
    C) 대
    D) 인

49) Match the Chinese character with its Korean pronunciation: 八
    A) 일
    B) 팔
    C) 이
    D) 인

50) Match the Chinese character with its Korean pronunciation: 山
    A) 이
    B) 오
    C) 이
    D) 산

51) Match the Chinese character with its Korean pronunciation: 中
    A) 중
    B) 오
    C) 이
    D) 산

52) Match the Chinese character with its Korean pronunciation: 三
    A) 삼
    B) 오
    C) 이
    D) 산

53) Match the Chinese character with its Korean pronunciation: 日
    A) 구
    B) 오
    C) 화
    D) 일

54) Match the Chinese character with its Korean pronunciation: 月
    A) 월
    B) 오
    C) 화
    D) 칠

55) Match the Chinese character with its Korean pronunciation: 七
    A) 중
    B) 십
    C) 소
    D) 칠

56) Match the Chinese character with its Korean pronunciation: 二

    A) 목
    B) 이
    C) 일
    D) 대

57) Match the Chinese character with its Korean pronunciation: 小

    A) 인
    B) 대
    C) 소
    D) 화

58) Match the Chinese character with its Korean pronunciation: 一

    A) 팔
    B) 구
    C) 수
    D) 일

59) Match the Chinese character with its Korean pronunciation: 火

    A) 사
    B) 이
    C) 화
    D) 인

60) Match the Chinese character with its Korean pronunciation: 五

A) 대
B) 육
C) 중
D) 오

Write the Korean pronunciation next to each character:

Chinese Character	Korean Pronunciation
61. 一	
62. 二	
63. 三	
64. 四	
65. 五	
66. 六	
67. 七	
68. 八	
69. 九	
70. 十	

71. 小	
72. 中	
73. 大	
74. 月	
75. 日	
76. 山	
77. 木	
78. 人	
79. 火	
80. 水	

Answer Key

1. One
2. Two
3. Three
4. Four
5. Five
6. Six
7. Seven
8. Eight
9. Nine
10. Ten
11. Seven
12. One
13. Two
14. Four
15. Five
16. Eight
17. Nine
18. Ten
19. Six
20. Three
21. B
22. C
23. A
24. D
25. B
26. B
27. D
28. B
29. B
30. D
31. A
32. B
33. B
34. D
35. B

36. C
37. C
38. B
39. B
40. A
41. D
42. C
43. A
44. A
45. C
46. A
47. C
48. B
49. B
50. D
51. A
52. A
53. D
54. A
55. D
56. B
57. C
58. D
59. C
60. D
61. 일
62. 이
63. 삼
64. 사
65. 오
66. 육
67. 칠
68. 팔
69. 구
70. 십

71. 소
72. 중
73. 대
74. 월
75. 일
76. 산
77. 목
78. 인
79. 화
80. 수

Printed in Poland
by Amazon Fulfillment
Poland Sp. z o.o., Wrocław